When Silence Looked Like Faith

Faith, healing, and the unseen blind spot in the church

Ginny Rucker

DEDICATION

This book is dedicated to my children.

To Marianna, who learned strength early, spoke truth with courage, and loved me with clarity when it mattered most.

To Jordan, who grew up watching resilience long before it was explained, and who carries both kindness and courage into the world.

You were never responsible for what I endured, but you were the reasons I kept going. Everything I did to survive was also done to protect you. Everything I did to heal was done so you could breathe easier too. This book exists because of you. It is written with the deepest love a mother can carry.

ACKNOWLEDGMENTS

This book is not the result of a crowd—it is the result of presence. First, I want to acknowledge God, whose nearness never depended on my clarity, my timing, or my strength. When I was confused, He was steady. When I was exhausted, He was patient. When I finally told the truth, He was not surprised. My faith did not survive because I held onto it perfectly, it survived because He never let go of me.

I acknowledge the few people who stood with me quietly – without needing explanation, without rushing my process, without asking me to soften what I lived through to make it easier to hear. You know who you are. Your steadiness mattered more than you may ever know.

I acknowledge the women whose stories intersect with mine—shared in whispers, messages, late night conversations, and tears. You confirmed that this book needed to exist. Your courage helped me trust my own truth.

And finally, I acknowledge myself.
For surviving without language.
For loving while afraid.
For staying longer than others understood.
For leaving when it finally became necessary.
For healing without an audience.
For telling the truth gently and firmly, without hatred.

This book is not the end of a story. It is evidence that truth, once spoken, can become a place of peace.

TABLE OF CONTENTS

AUTHOR'S NOTE

I didn't set out to write this book. For a long time, I carried my story quietly—not because it didn't matter, but because I believed silence was part of faithfulness. I believed endurance was evidence of love. I believed protecting others from discomfort was part of my responsibility.

What changed wasn't my faith. What changed was my understanding of what faith was never meant to require.

This book was born out of a realization that came slowly and painfully: my story was not unique. As I began speaking more honestly about what I had lived through, other women found me. Different ages. Different churches. Different marriages. The details varied, but the patterns did not. And neither did the responses they received when they asked for help.

This is not a book written in anger; it is written in grief, clarity, and hope.

I love the church. I have served in it. I still do. I believe deeply in its mission, its calling, and its potential to be one of the safest places on earth for people in crisis. But love tells the truth when something is not working. Love names blind spots not to shame, but to strengthen.

This book is not an indictment of pastors, leaders, or faith communities.

It is an invitation.

An invitation to learn what many churches were never taught: how abuse actually presents inside marriage, how coercive control hides behind respectability, how spiritual language can be misused without malicious intent, and how silence—when untrained—can cause harm even when compassion is present.

I share my story not because it is the worst, but because it is recognizable.

If you are a survivor, my hope is that these pages give language to things you may have felt but never named. That you recognize yourself without being retraumatized. That you feel less alone, less confused, and less pressured to rush your own timeline.

If you are a church leader, my hope is that this book expands—not diminishes—your capacity to care. That it offers clarity where there has been discomfort. That it equips you with understanding rather than blame. That it helps you respond sooner, safer, and with confidence when someone trusts you with their truth.

This book sits at the intersection of story and education because both are necessary. My aim is not to tell the church what it has done wrong—but to help it do better.

If this book helps even one woman recognize danger sooner or helps one leader respond with clarity instead of confusion, then telling the truth was worth it.

Thank you for reading with an open heart.

— Ginny

INTRODUCTION

I didn't leave my marriage because I stopped believing in God.

I left because I finally understood God never asked me to stay and disappear inside it.

For years, the church knew my husband as a leader—confident, dependable, articulate in faith. He served publicly, photographed ministry events, and welcomed people with ease. They trusted him long before anyone realized he would use the same spiritual language to shame, silence, and control me privately. His abuse was not loud in the ways churches are trained to recognize. It was quiet, constant, and calculated—primarily verbal, psychological, financial, and spiritual. There was physical abuse as well, but not in the way people expect. No closed fists to my face. Instead, intimidation. Blocking exits. Grabbing arms and slamming my body against the wall. Looming presence. Fear that lived in proximity rather than a black eye.

And that was the problem. I was in pain, but not in proof.

When I reached out for help, I was met not with cruelty, but with uncertainty. Discomfort. Spiritual advice offered without safety. Words like submit, pray harder, and be patient—spoken gently, but leaving me alone in danger.

Churches know how to respond to visible suffering.

They feed the hungry. Shelter the homeless. Support addiction recovery. And that work is needed. But when suffering lives inside a marriage—inside a home, a mind, a nervous system—when the bruises don't show, many churches quietly step back.

Not because they lack compassion.

But because they lack training.

I'm not writing this book to shame the church. I'm writing it to strengthen it. Because every ministry trained to respond to hunger should also know how to respond to abuse. Every leader equipped to mobilize aid should also know how to recognize coercive control. And every woman should be believed before she is visibly broken.

This book exists to change the curriculum, not the faith.

If you are a survivor who felt unseen in a place meant to be safe, this book is for you.

If you are a church leader who genuinely didn't know what to do—but wants to know now—this book is for you too.

Because abuse doesn't require visible wounds to be real.

And faith should never require a woman to bleed silently to be believed.

PART ONE – WHEN SAFETY FELT LIKE LOVE

"So do not fear, for I am with you; do not be dismayed, for I am your God. I will strengthen you and help you; I will uphold you with my righteous right hand."
— Isaiah 41:10

CHAPTER ONE – I TRUSTED WHAT FELT LIKE PROTECTION

I was thirty when I met him, already living a life shaped by responsibility. My son was eleven, my daughter was nine, and the three of us had learned how to be a family without anyone else filling the gaps. Single motherhood had made me steady. It taught me how to solve problems quietly, how to anticipate needs before they became emergencies, how to smile through weight without asking for help. My life wasn't perfect, but it was honest. I knew who I was. I knew what safety felt like.

He entered my life in July of 2005 with confidence that felt grounding. Not flashy. Not loud. Just sure. He spoke directly. He listened attentively. He paid attention to my children in ways that felt respectful, not performative. When tension arose with my controlling family, he stepped in without hesitation and defended me. I remember thinking, "This is what partnership looks like. This is what covering feels like." What I didn't know then was how easily confidence can masquerade as protection when you've spent years protecting yourself.

We weren't in the church when we met. Faith existed in some fashion, but it wasn't yet structured around Sunday mornings or ministry calendars, and a relationship with Jesus hadn't been established yet. That changed in October of 2006. We started attending church together, and in that same month, I found out I was pregnant. Another son. A new life arriving in a season already heavy with transition.

Not long after, one day without warning, he said,

"We need to go to the church."
I looked up from what I was doing. "Now?"
"Yes. We need to talk to a pastor. We need to get married."

There was no proposal. No question. Just direction. The drive there was quiet in a way that didn't invite conversation.

When we arrived, he walked straight to the front desk and asked to see a pastor immediately. We were ushered into a small office where he explained our situation plainly. We were expecting a child. We needed to be married.

The pastor listened kindly. He didn't ask how we had decided this. He didn't ask if I felt ready. He didn't ask about the relationship beyond willingness. And in that moment, willingness felt like the same thing as intention.

I smiled. I nodded. I believed this was commitment taking shape.

We married in February of 2007. From the outside, it looked like a story coming together the right way—faith, family, responsibility, structure. I believed marriage would solidify what already felt good. I believed covenant would bring calm.

I didn't yet understand that covenant doesn't change character.
It reveals it.

The first crack appeared days after the wedding, quietly, in the kitchen. One of the kids had left a cupboard door open. A small thing. A child thing. He reacted with an intensity that didn't match the moment. He raised his voice. He moved close enough that my body stiffened before my thoughts caught up. He spoke about disrespect. Disorder. Leadership. "It's not a big deal, I'll close it," I said, confused at this reaction. He grabbed his keys and told me maybe he shouldn't have married me. That maybe this was a mistake. Then he left the house.

He came back later. But something didn't. What stayed with me wasn't the argument. It was the realization that conflict wouldn't always lead to repair. That love might be conditional with this person. That safety might depend on how well I adapted. I didn't name it then. I just filed it away.

By the end of that first chapter of our life together, I wasn't afraid.

But I was no longer at ease.

And that difference matters.

CHAPTER TWO — LIFE LOOKED WHOLE

After we started attending church, ministry became part of my life naturally. Not immediately, and not as a title, but as service. Hospitality was where I began—welcoming families, organizing spaces, preparing food, coordinating volunteers. It felt familiar. Creating order and warmth had always been how I loved people. Then children's ministry followed. I understood children. I knew how to kneel down, make eye contact, explain God without fear. I taught lessons, helped with crafts, prayed with kids who were anxious or overwhelmed. I told them God saw them and loved them and cared about how they felt. I meant every word.

As the years passed, youth ministry came next. Then young adult ministry. I organized events, mentored teens, listened to college-age kids trying to navigate faith, identity, and relationships. I was steady. Available. Safe. People began calling me Mama G. I smiled at the name, unaware that I had already started living into it—absorbing turbulence so others didn't have to.

His ministry role was visible. The first year, he ushered. After that, photography became his place. He documented events, outreaches, baptisms. People recognized him. Trusted him. Associated him with generosity and service.

From the outside, we looked like a family doing everything right. Inside the marriage, something was tightening. Not suddenly. Gradually.

Conversations became minefields. Tone mattered more than content. Questions were interpreted as challenges. Silence was read as defiance. Scripture entered arguments not as comfort, but as control. I found myself working harder to get things right instead of asking whether things were safe.

I adjusted constantly. My voice softened. My words shortened. My instincts learned to pause before speaking. I smiled more. I served harder. And I still believed this was what commitment required.

Three years into the marriage, the exhaustion had settled somewhere deep. I wasn't desperate yet—just unsettled. I didn't have language for what was happening. I only knew I was shrinking, and shrinking felt wrong.

I reached out to a counselor within the church. Someone positioned to help couples navigate difficulty. I explained it carefully—the yelling, the control, the way scripture felt twisted, the way I was always adapting.

They listened. Then they asked, "What are you doing to make him do these things to you? Are you really trying to be a good, godly wife?"

I remember blinking, the room suddenly too bright. "I'm trying," I said quietly. "I just feel like I'm disappearing." They encouraged prayer, submission, and patience. I left with spiritual homework instead of safety.

Still hopeful.

Still faithful.

Still smiling.

At home, nothing changed. In ministry, everything looked fine. People praised my resilience. Pastors referenced my smile. No one questioned the cost.

- I didn't yet know that strength can become camouflage for harm.
- I didn't yet know that systems often preserve appearance before they learn how to protect people.
- I didn't yet know that asking for help early can sometimes leave you more alone.
- I only knew that something inside me was whispering **This** isn't what love is supposed to feel like.

And that whisper was getting harder to ignore.

CHAPTER THREE – ENDURANCE WAS REPLACING DISCERNMENT

In long marriages that no longer feel safe, you reach a moment when you realize you are no longer reacting—you are anticipating.

I didn't wake up one day afraid. I woke up prepared.

- Prepared to choose my words carefully.
- Prepared to read tone before content.
- Prepared to adjust my posture, my timing, my silence.
- Prepared to manage emotional weather before it became a storm.

That preparation felt like maturity at first—growth, wisdom, marriage muscles strengthening. But discernment doesn't require you to disappear. And endurance does not require you to live on edge. I didn't know the distinction yet—but my body did.

On paper, life looked full. Ministry schedules. School calendars. Youth events. Church services. Family dinners. A growing household with children at different stages and responsibilities layered on top of one another. At home, the tension wasn't constant—and that was part of the confusion.

There were good days. Laughter. Moments that felt almost normal. Enough kindness to make me doubt myself when the atmosphere shifted again. But unpredictability became the constant.

I never knew which version of him I was coming home to. The calm one. The critical one. The silent one. The violent one. The one who needed control more than connection. And because there was no visible pattern to outsiders, I became the stabilizer.

I learned how to soften conversations before they hardened. How to apologize even when I wasn't wrong. How to absorb emotional force so it wouldn't land on the kids. I became a buffer long before I became aware of the cost. I told myself the kids were protected. And in some ways, they were. I shielded them from the worst moments. I redirected arguments. I took the brunt of the emotional fallout. But children don't need to hear everything to feel something. They felt the shift in energy. They noticed when rooms went quiet too quickly. They watched how often I smiled after crying privately. They adapted too.

People commented on my smile constantly. "You're always smiling." "You're so strong." "I don't know how you do it." The smile wasn't denial. It was adaptation. It kept rooms calm. It kept questions away. It kept me functioning.

Scripture, once a refuge, began to feel heavy. Verses were used to correct my posture instead of cover my heart. Submission was emphasized more than gentleness. Leadership more than mutuality.

I didn't stop loving God. I started wondering why loving God felt like it required me to lose myself. I reasoned my way through pain: It's not that bad. Marriage is hard. At least he doesn't hit me in the face.

There were moments of physical abuse and intimidation—blocking exits, grabbing arms, slamming me against the wall, and looming presence—but because it didn't look like what I'd been taught to fear, I minimized it.

Something in me began to wake up. I started noticing how tired I felt even after rest. How my body stayed tense in quiet rooms. How peace felt foreign. That awareness didn't make me leave. It made me pause.

And sometimes, pause is the most dangerous thing for systems that depend on your silence.

FOR CHURCH LEADERS –

What This Chapter Is Asking You to Learn

Abuse does not begin with violence. It begins with control, intimidation, and fear of consequences.

If a man blocks exits, grabs arms, looms physically, corners his spouse, or uses proximity to intimidate, that is physical abuse, even if he never closes a fist or leaves a visible bruise. Minimizing harm because it does not meet a dramatic threshold keeps survivors trapped inside technicalities instead of protected by truth.

Churches are often trained to look for explosions. Abuse more often looks like erosion.

When a woman becomes quieter, more careful, more apologetic, more "reasonable," more accommodating—that is not spiritual maturity. That is often a nervous system adapting to danger.

If a survivor sounds calm, articulate, faithful, and controlled while describing harm, do not assume safety. Assume practice.

Churches must learn to ask:
- Who is adapting, and why?
- Who carries the emotional weight so others don't have to?
- What patterns repeat when no one is watching?

Ministry visibility is not evidence of character.

Endurance is not evidence of consent.

And submission is never meant to require fear.

FOR SURVIVORS –

If This Chapter Felt Familiar

If you told yourself, it wasn't abuse because he didn't hit you "hard enough," because he didn't hit you "often," because he didn't hit you "the way people expect," you are not minimizing — you were surviving.

Physical abuse includes intimidation, restraint, blocking, grabbing, looming, and using the body as a weapon without a punch. Your body knows the difference, even when language comes later.

If you became careful instead of loud, accommodating instead of confrontational, smiling instead of honest —that does not mean you were weak. It means your nervous system learned how to keep you alive.

You are not dramatic for feeling unsafe.
You are not disobedient for noticing fear.
You are not faithless for questioning an environment that required you to shrink.

Awareness is not rebellion; it is the beginning of truth.

And if you recognize yourself here, know this:

You didn't fail marriage.

Marriage failed to protect you.

PART TWO – WHEN THE TRUTH FOUND ME

"Then you will know the truth, and the truth will set you free."
— John 8:32

CHAPTER FOUR – WHEN LANGUAGE FINALLY CAME

Awareness is unsettling when it first arrives—not because it's loud, but because it refuses to be ignored. By 2016, the strain was no longer just emotional. My body carried it. Sleep came lightly. My heart raced during conversations that shouldn't have required adrenaline.

When he agreed to marital counseling, I didn't feel hopeful so much as relieved. Not because I believed counseling would fix everything, but because I believed someone else might finally see what I had been living with alone.

Our counselor was a psychologist. Trained to listen for patterns, not personalities. For six months, we sat in that office together. He spoke confidently. Persuasively. I explained myself carefully. Near the end of those sessions, I went alone. The counselor looked at me and said, "I'm glad you're here by yourself. I'm worried about your safety—and I fear for your life." The words rearranged everything. He finally gave language to what I had been living for years: narcissism, coercive control, psychological dominance, intimidation that didn't require bruises to be dangerous. For the first time, I wasn't being asked what I was doing wrong; I was being told the environment itself was unsafe.

Not long after, I moved into the guest room.
From the outside, it looked small.
From the inside, it was seismic.

That space became the first place where my nervous system could unclench. I was still in the marriage. Still in the house. Still smiling. But I was no longer pretending this was normal. I began praying differently. "God, reveal the truth." Not to punish. Not to expose, but to bring clarity where confusion had lived too long. I didn't know yet how long that prayer would take to answer. But I knew this:

Naming it didn't end it.

It changed me.

FOR CHURCH LEADERS –

What This Chapter Requires You to Understand

- When a trained clinician names abuse, it should never be overridden by spiritual platitudes. If a psychologist identifies coercive control, intimidation, and narcissistic behavior, the church's role is not to reinterpret it—but to respond responsibly.
- Physical abuse is not defined by fists alone.
- Blocking, grabbing, looming, cornering, slamming against the wall and a threatening presence are all physical expressions of control.
- When a survivor moves into another room instead of leaving the marriage, do not interpret that as avoidance or immaturity. It may be the first boundary she has ever been allowed to draw safely.

Churches must learn the difference between:
- Conflict and coercive control.
- Marital strain and psychological danger.
- Submission and silence.
- Patience and survival.

Education does not weaken the church; it protects it from causing harm unintentionally.

FOR SURVIVORS –

If This Chapter Gave You Language

If someone finally named what you've been living in and it felt like relief instead of fear, that is not betrayal. It is clarity.

If you minimized physical abuse because it didn't look the way you were taught it should, you are not naïve—you were navigating danger without vocabulary.

If creating space felt like the only way you could breathe, that does not make you dramatic or disobedient. It makes you self-protective.

Awareness does not force action. It prepares you for it.
And you are allowed to take that preparation one step at a time.

CHAPTER FIVE – STAYING DIDN'T MEAN I WAS CONFUSED

By the time clarity arrived, leaving was no longer a simple decision. I understood what I was living in now. I finally had language for what I was living in. I had validation from a professional who had seen the pattern clearly. I had drawn a boundary inside the house that gave my body a little space to breathe. But understanding does not automatically remove obligation, and obligation was about to multiply.

In early 2020, I began quietly preparing myself to leave. Not dramatically. Not publicly. Just internally—the way most women in long marriages do when they know something must eventually change. I prayed. I planned. I waited for the right moment.

Then the world shut down.

COVID didn't create the crisis in my home, but it trapped me inside it more tightly. Schools closed. Schedules collapsed. Resources narrowed. Every plan I had made became harder to execute, not because I doubted myself, but because circumstances closed in all at once.

In September, everything shifted again. He was diagnosed with kidney cancer. Suddenly the house filled with appointments, scans, procedures, and conversations with doctors. He lost a kidney. Recovery became the new priority. And without discussion, I stepped into the role I had always stepped into when crisis arrived…Caregiver.

Not because I forgot what I had learned. Not because I believed the abuse had ended. I stayed because compassion and clarity can coexist in complicated ways.

I stayed.

For a moment, I wondered if illness would soften him. If facing mortality would shift something fundamental. It did not.

The criticism continued. The control adapted. The expectation that I would absorb everything without complaint only intensified. Then, two days after Christmas, he had a severe stroke. Hospital rooms. ICU monitors. Rehabilitation centers. Months of recovery. I coordinated medications, appointments, therapies, and schedules. I protected the kids from fear while containing my own. My adult daughter watched closely now. My teenage son absorbed tension he didn't yet know how to articulate. I was exhausted beyond tired. My body was running on adrenaline it had been using for years.

And still I stayed.

People often asked later, "Why didn't you leave then?" The answer is not simple, but it is honest:

- I didn't stay because I was stupid.
- I didn't stay because I lacked faith.
- I didn't stay because I didn't understand the danger.
    - I stayed because I was carrying too many lives at once.
    - I was a wife to a sick man.
    - A mother to children who needed stability.
    - A caregiver during a global crisis.
    - A woman with clarity but limited options.

Leaving in that moment would have meant detonating every fragile structure at the same time. And I was still trying to hold the family together long enough for everyone else to land safely.

Endurance is not always confusion; sometimes it's triage.

One of the hardest truths I had to accept during this season was this: illness did not excuse abuse. It complicated escape, but it did not cancel harm. Even during recovery, the intimidation remained. The proximity. The tone. The physical presence that blocked, loomed, and reminded me where he believed power lived. He insisted it was not physical abuse because he never closed his fist or hit my face. But my body did not need bruises to know the truth. Fear does not require visible injury to be valid. I had already learned that. Now I was living it with exhaustion layered on top.

My prayers shifted again during this season. They were no longer only about truth being revealed. They were about survival without self-erasure. "God, help me do this without losing myself." I did not know then how long it would take. I only knew I could not stay forever.

FOR CHURCH LEADERS –

What This Chapter Asks You to Learn

<u>Illness does not cancel abuse.</u>

It often intensifies dependence, making escape more dangerous and more complex. When a survivor stays during a spouse's illness, it should not be interpreted as reconciliation, denial, or consent. It may be compassion layered on top of fear, responsibility, and limited options.

- Caretaking does not equal safety.
- Endurance does not equal agreement.

Churches must learn to recognize triage seasons, where a woman may understand the danger clearly but cannot yet leave without significant risk to herself or her children.

Asking "why didn't you leave?" in these moments causes harm. The better questions are:

- What support would make leaving safer later?
- How can we reduce her isolation now?
- How do we protect children who are watching silently?

FOR SURVIVORS –

If You Stayed Longer Than You Planned

1. If you stayed through illness, crisis, or caregiving after clarity arrived, you are not weak.
   a. You were managing competing responsibilities with limited support.
2. If your compassion was used against you, that does not make compassion a flaw.
   a. It means it was exploited.

You are allowed to honor the care you gave without staying in the environment that required it forever. Leaving does not erase the love you showed. And staying does not invalidate the truth you learned.

Both can be true.

CHAPTER SIX – WHEN I FINALLY SPOKE OUT LOUD

There is a particular kind of loneliness that comes from knowing the truth and still having nowhere safe to put it. By the time I spoke out loud again, I wasn't confused anymore. I wasn't dramatic. I wasn't searching for attention or validation. I had already sat with the reality of my marriage in private for years. I had done the work of naming it internally. I had adjusted my expectations, my boundaries, and my prayers.

What I needed now wasn't an explanation. It was support.

Between 2020 and 2022, I reached out to the church again—this time not to a counselor, but to a pastor's wife at a different church than the one we had started in. I chose her intentionally. She was someone I believed would understand both faith and complexity. Someone who had proximity to leadership but also the relational authority to respond with care.

- I did not arrive angry.
- I did not arrive accusatory.
- I arrived tired.

I explained carefully. Measured. I spoke about the control, the volatility, the intimidation, the infidelity. I named the fear without exaggeration. I did not unload everything at once. I watched her face closely, gauging whether it was safe to keep going.

At first, she was kind. She listened. She nodded. She said she was sorry I was going through so much. Her voice carried concern, and for a moment, I felt that familiar relief—the kind that comes when someone finally believes you, even if they don't yet know what to do. That moment mattered more than she probably realized.

But kindness without capacity has a shelf life.

As time passed and the situation didn't resolve itself neatly, the posture shifted. I could feel it in the way conversations shortened. In the way responses became less curious and more closed. In the way discomfort replaced concern.

One day, as I began explaining another incident—slowly, carefully, choosing my words—she stopped me. "I don't want to hear anything else about it," she said. The words weren't sharp. They weren't cruel. They were final. Later, she told me she would just be praying for me. And then came the question that landed heavier than anything else she said: "If it's really that bad…why haven't you left yet? Why haven't you done anything up until now?" The question wasn't asked to understand; It was asked to create distance. In that moment, the responsibility shifted back onto me—not for surviving, but for not having escaped sooner. Not for being harmed, but for still being there. I felt something close inside me. Not anger. Recognition.

My daughter had been watching all of this unfold for years. She was no longer a child protected by redirection. She was an adult who could see clearly, and what she saw frightened her. The instability. The control. The toll it was taking on my body and spirit. She reached out to the pastor's wife herself. She told her she was afraid for my safety. That was not enough to reopen the door.

The response was brief. Spiritual. Detached. And in that moment, I understood something that was painful but clarifying:

This was not about cruelty; it was about capacity.

They did not know what to do with abuse that didn't arrive bleeding or shouting. They did not know how to hold a situation that required action instead of prayer alone. And rather than admit that, they stepped back. I was not rejected with anger; I was dismissed with discomfort.

I did not leave the marriage immediately after that. But I did leave the church.

Not in bitterness.

Not in rebellion.

But in clarity.

I realized I could not continue worshiping in a place that required my silence, in order to remain comfortable. I could not keep serving in a system that was unprepared to protect women and children when harm lived quietly behind respectable roles.

Walking away from that church hurt—not because I lost faith, but because I lost the illusion that faith communities always know how to respond when abuse doesn't look the way they expect.

Later, after I finally left the marriage, people from throughout the years told me things I wish I had never had to carry.

"We knew something was off."

"He was unstable."

"We saw signs."

And when I reached out, I was met with prayer without presence, questions without protection, and silence that was framed as wisdom. That truth didn't make me angry. It made me determined. Because if people could recognize instability after the fact, they could be trained to recognize it before damage compounds. And because no woman should have to choose between faith and safety.

FOR CHURCH LEADERS –

What This Chapter Requires You to Face

<u>Silence is not neutrality.</u>

When leaders respond with prayer alone in situations of domestic abuse, they are not staying spiritual—they are staying untrained.

Asking "why haven't you left yet?" places responsibility on the survivor instead of examining the danger, complexity, and risk involved in leaving.

Churches must learn to:

- Recognize abuse without visible injury.
- Respond to disclosure with action plans, not distancing.
- Treat domestic abuse as a crisis, not a character issue.
- Understand that prayer without protection can retraumatize.
- If a daughter reaches out saying she fears for her mother's safety, that is not gossip. That is a warning.

FOR SURVIVORS –

If Speaking Up Cost You Community

1. If you spoke up and were met with prayer instead of help.
    a. You are not unworthy of support.
2. If your disclosure made people uncomfortable enough to step back.
    a. That does not mean you were wrong to speak.
3. If you lost community before you left the marriage.
    a. You did not fail.
        i. You outgrew silence.

Sometimes the bravest thing a woman does is tell the truth and accept that not everyone is equipped to stand with her once they hear it…But someone will be.

Your voice matters enough to keep speaking until that support exists.

CHAPTER SEVEN – QUIET EXIT, LOUD OPINIONS

I did not leave in the way people expect women to leave abusive marriages. There was no dramatic argument that finally crossed a visible line. No police. No emergency bag packed in the night. No announcement to leadership. No moment that would have made sense to people who believe clarity always arrives loudly. The decision came quietly—after years of noise had already taken up residence inside my body.

By October of 2023, I knew with a certainty that didn't need validation that I could not continue living this way. Not because I suddenly lacked compassion. Not because I stopped believing in restoration. Not because I had hardened my heart. But because survival had become the baseline. And survival is not the same thing as living. I stayed in the house. He moved out. That detail matters. I did not flee. I did not abandon my children's home. I did not run from responsibility. I chose stability for my kids and distance from harm at the same time.

The circle I made that decision with was small: God, my adult daughter, and my teenage son. That was it. No committee. No church leadership. No safety net beyond the people who had lived inside the reality with me long enough to understand the cost. For years, I had buffered my children from the worst of the abuse. Redirected tension. Absorbed emotional fallout. Took the brunt so they could stay children longer than the environment would have otherwise allowed. Now they were standing beside me—not because they were asked to choose sides, but because they already knew the truth.

The backlash came faster than the peace. Some people didn't believe me at all. They were stunned by the idea that a man who had served faithfully, who held a camera for ministry outreaches, who showed up consistently, who smiled easily and helped publicly, could ever be the same man who controlled, belittled, intimidated, or harmed a wife privately.

"There's no way."
"He's so nice."
"He served in church."
"You must be exaggerating."
"I never saw that side of him."

Others responded differently.

"We suspected something."
"We saw instability."
"I'm sorry you went through that alone."

Two opposite reactions, born from the same failure—a system that didn't know how to see abuse unless it arrived loudly and visibly. The backlash wasn't always cruel. Often, it was confusion dressed up as certainty. People wanted a version of events that fit comfortably inside what they already believed. And I no longer had the energy to help them reconcile that.

People assume leaving brings immediate relief. It didn't. At first, my body collapsed. Years of living in fight-or-flight had rewired my nervous system. When the danger finally moved out of the house, my body didn't celebrate. It crashed.

I slept constantly.

Not depression—depletion.

My muscles ached. My breath felt shallow even in quiet rooms. Tears came without warning. My heart raced for reasons I couldn't always name. My body was finally doing what it had never been allowed to do before.

Stop bracing.

Years of adrenaline had kept me functional. When the threat was gone, my system no longer needed to hold itself upright. It needed to recover. That kind of healing is not pretty. It is biological. It is slow. It requires rest without guilt and tears without explanation. And I did it without a church community.

Just my kids. Just God.

Only after the backlash quieted did healing begin to take shape. Counseling helped me understand how deeply my nervous system had been conditioned by years of unpredictability. How constant vigilance had become normal. How peace had to be relearned. My son entered counseling too, processing the impact of living in an environment where tension had been the background noise of childhood. We learned new rhythms together. Quieter ones. Slower ones. Rhythms that did not require scanning rooms or measuring tone.

Socially, my world became smaller—and healthier. I stepped back from people who needed me to doubt myself in order to stay comfortable. I didn't argue. I didn't defend myself. I simply stopped offering my energy to conversations that required me to minimize my truth. I leaned into the few who showed up quietly and consistently. They didn't demand explanations. They didn't ask for proof. They trusted me because they knew my character, not because they had witnessed my pain.

Spiritually, I rebuilt not from scratch, but from memory. God had never left. Jesus had been present through every season—when I was confused, when I was surviving, when I was finally choosing peace.

I still loved ministry. I still believed in the church., but I now believed it could—and must—do better.

FOR CHURCH LEADERS –

What This Chapter Makes Clear

1. When a survivor leaves quietly, do not assume the harm was quiet. The absence of chaos often means the decision was made after long consideration, fear, and exhaustion—not impulsivity.
2. Backlash harms survivors most before healing begins. Disbelief, minimization, and social pressure can retraumatize women at the most vulnerable point in their journey.
3. Ministry serving does not make abuse impossible.
4. Niceness does not negate harm.
5. Visibility does not equal accountability.

Churches must learn to respond to disclosure with humility instead of defense, and support instead of skepticism.

FOR SURVIVORS –

If Leaving Didn't Feel Like Freedom Right Away

- If your body collapsed after you left:
  - You are not broken.
    - You are decompressing.
- If Peace felt unfamiliar at first:
  - That doesn't mean you made the wrong decision.
    - It means your nervous system is relearning safety.

You don't owe anyone an explanation that costs you your healing.
Leaving quietly does not make your story smaller.
It makes it truer.

PART THREE – WHAT JUSTICE, MERCY, AND HUMILITY REQUIRE

"He has shown you, O man, what is good; and what does the Lord require of you but to do justice, to love mercy, and to walk humbly with your God."
— Micah 6:8

CHAPTER EIGHT – LIVING WITHOUT BRACING

Peace did not arrive all at once. It arrived in fragments. A morning where the house stayed quiet longer than expected. A conversation that didn't require rehearsal. A moment when my shoulders dropped without permission. For years, calm had been temporary. Silence meant something was coming. Stillness was something to monitor, not trust. My body had learned that safety was conditional and always revocable. So, when the house remained calm after he moved out, my nervous system didn't relax. It waited.

Healing, I learned, does not begin with relief. It begins with disbelief.

When the Body Learns Before the Mind.

I knew, intellectually, that the danger was gone. My body did not believe me. I slept deeply and constantly, as if my system was trying to make up for years of vigilance all at once. My muscles ached. My heart raced without clear triggers. Tears came without context. Ordinary sounds startled me. Quiet felt foreign.

This was not weakness. It was biology. Years of living in fight-or-flight had kept me functional. Adrenaline had been my fuel. When survival was no longer required, my nervous system didn't know how to stand down. Counseling helped me understand this. Not as pathology, but as recovery. My body wasn't breaking down—it was recalibrating. My children were doing the same. Each of us carried different memories, different adaptations, different grief. Healing did not look identical in our home, but it moved in the same direction.

Toward safety.

Toward honesty.

Toward rest.

Rebuilding Without Explaining

I stepped back from people who needed me to question my own reality, in order to preserve theirs. I didn't argue. I didn't correct misconceptions. I didn't defend my timeline. I simply stopped offering myself to conversations that required me to shrink in order to be accepted. At the same time, I leaned into the few people who showed up without conditions. They didn't need details. They didn't ask for proof. They didn't want a version of the story that made them comfortable. They trusted me. That mattered more than numbers. Rebuilding my identity didn't come through reinvention. It came through remembering. Remembering who I was before survival became my primary skill. Remembering what peace felt like. Remembering that I did not need to earn safety by being agreeable or endlessly strong.

Faith Without Performance

Spiritually, I rebuilt slowly. Not through leadership roles. Not through visibility. Not through service that demanded strength I didn't yet have. I rebuilt through quiet prayer. Through scripture read without pressure. Through the realization that Jesus had never left—not during the confusion, not during the endurance, not during the silence. He had been present the entire time. Not as an enforcer of submission. Not as a judge of my decisions. But as a steady presence when I didn't know how to survive without shrinking.

I was not angry at the church. I was disappointed. And disappointment is not the opposite of faith—it is often the beginning of discernment. I still loved ministry. I still believed in the church. But I now believed it could— and must—become safer.

When Other Women Started Finding Me

During this season of rebuilding, something unexpected happened. Women began finding me. Quietly. Privately. Carefully. Their stories weren't identical to mine. Different marriages. Different churches. Different circumstances. But the pattern was unmistakable. Verbal control. Spiritual distortion. Minimization of harm. Questions that shifted responsibility back onto them. Prayer offered without protection. Silence justified as wisdom. I realized then that this book was not just personal. It was necessary. Not to accuse the church—but to educate it. Not to shame leaders—but to equip them. Not to relive pain—but to prevent it where possible.

The Smile That Changed Meaning

People still comment on my smile. But now it comes from peace, not pressure. From choice, not endurance. From joy that does not require explanation. I smile because my home is quiet. Because my children breathe easier. Because my body is learning how to rest. Because my faith survived honesty. Because my voice no longer needs permission.

FOR CHURCH LEADERS –

What This Chapter Is Asking You to See

1. Healing after abuse is layered, biological, and often invisible.
2. When a survivor leaves, your responsibility does not end—it shifts.
    a. Support after exit matters as much as response during disclosure.
3. If multiple women tell similar stories, that is not coincidence. It is a pattern asking for education.

Churches must move beyond good intentions and develop training:
- Clear response protocols
- Referral pathways
- Trauma-informed language
- Safety-first frameworks

The goal is not perfection; the goal is preparedness.

FOR SURVIVORS –

If You Are Rebuilding Quietly

- If your world feels smaller after leaving.
  - That does not mean you failed.
    - It means you chose health over noise.
- If healing feels slow or uneven.
  - Your body is doing exactly what it needs to do.
    - You are not behind. You are recovering.

You are allowed to love faith without returning to harm.
You are allowed to smile without proving anything.

You are allowed to tell your story—not because you owe it to anyone, but because it may help someone else recognize themselves sooner than you were allowed to.

CHAPTER NINE – THE BLIND SPOT ISN'T MALICE.

IT'S TRAINING

By the time I understood my story wasn't isolated, I had stopped asking why this happened to me. The more urgent question became: Why does this keep happening to so many women inside the church?

Not quietly. Not occasionally. But predictably. I began noticing the same pattern repeating across denominations, worship styles, leadership structures, and theology. Different churches. Different leaders. Different women. The same response. Concern at first. Discomfort soon after. Distance when the story didn't resolve quickly. It wasn't cruelty. It wasn't indifference. And it wasn't conspiracy. It was a blind spot.

The Church Is Excellent at What It Can See

Churches know how to mobilize around visible crises. Homelessness has outreach teams. Addiction has recovery programs. Food insecurity has pantries. Grief has casseroles, prayer chains, and cards. These are good things. Necessary things. Faithful things. But domestic abuse doesn't announce itself. It doesn't show up hungry. It doesn't show up intoxicated; it doesn't show up with police reports most of the time. It shows up early to serve. It shows up composed. It shows up smiling. It shows up exhausted but faithful.

And because the church is trained to respond to visible collapse, it often misses invisible coercion.

Why Abuse Inside Marriage Feels "Too Complicated"

Abuse inside marriage asks the church to do something uncomfortable. It asks leaders to:
- Hold tension instead of resolving it quickly.
- Prioritize safety without demonizing.
- Believe a woman without demanding spectacle.

- Act without perfect clarity.
- That discomfort often leads to spiritual bypassing.

"Pray more."
"Submit better."
"Be patient."
"Give it time."

These phrases are rarely meant to harm. But when used in situations of coercive control, they function as silencers rather than supports. The truth is this: many churches were never trained to respond to abuse without becoming investigators or judges. So, they choose distance instead. Distance feels safer than responsibility.

When Niceness Becomes a Shield

One of the most dangerous myths in church culture is the belief that character is proven by public service. Niceness becomes synonymous with safety. Visibility becomes synonymous with accountability. Ministry involvement becomes synonymous with maturity. But abuse does not disqualify itself because a man serves well publicly. In fact, systems that reward reliability, charm, and consistency can unintentionally protect those who know how to perform stability while controlling privately. The issue isn't that churches believe abusers—it's that they haven't been trained to question patterns over presentation.

The Cost of Not Knowing

When churches don't know how to respond to domestic abuse, the cost is high. Women stop disclosing. Children learn silence as safety. Leaders carry regret after the fact. Faith communities lose credibility with the very people they are meant to protect. I've had leaders apologize to me years later. Sincerely. Humbly. But apology after harm does not replace preparation before it.

This Was Never About Blame

I am not interested in indicting the church. I am interested in educating it. Because ignorance is not neutral when lives are at stake. And systems don't become safer by accident. They become safer because someone names the gap and refuses to pretend it doesn't exist.

FOR CHURCH LEADERS –

What This Chapter Is Calling You Toward

The church does not need to become law enforcement. It needs to become literate in abuse dynamics.

Domestic abuse training should be as standard as:
- Child protection checks
- Background checks
- Addiction response protocols

Leaders must learn to recognize:
- Coercive control.
- Intimidation without bruises.
- Spiritual language used as dominance.
- Nervous system distress disguised as strength.

Good intentions are not enough. Competence protects compassion.

FOR SURVIVORS –

If the Church Didn't Know What to Do with Your Truth

If your disclosure was met with confusion, distance, or prayer without protection, you are not imagining the gap.

- You encountered a system that was untrained—not a God who was absent.
- Your story mattered even if it wasn't handled well.
- Your safety mattered even if it wasn't prioritized correctly.
- Your faith is still valid even if the response failed you.
- You did not ask for too much.

You asked the right questions in a place that didn't yet know how to answer them.

CHAPTER TEN – GOOD INTENTIONS ARE NOT A SAFETY PLAN

If the church wants to do better, it has to stop relying on instinct alone. Most harm in abuse cases does not come from cruelty; it comes from unpreparedness. From leaders who care deeply but have never been taught what to do when a woman sits across from them and says, "Something isn't right in my marriage." The church is not failing because it lacks compassion; it is failing because compassion without structure collapses under pressure.

What Often Happens Instead of What Is Needed

When a survivor discloses abuse, churches often respond with one of three instincts.

- Spiritualization:
  - Encouraging prayer, patience, submission, or forgiveness before safety is assessed.
- Minimization:
  - Reframing abuse as "marital conflict," "communication issues," or "stress."
- Distance:
  - Offering prayer without presence. Stepping back once the situation becomes complex or uncomfortable.

These responses are understandable. They are also not neutral. They shift responsibility back onto the survivor. They delay intervention. They reinforce silence. And silence is where abuse thrives.

The Questions That Quietly Cause Harm

Many women remember the exact moment they stopped asking for help.
It usually sounds like this:

"What are you doing to make him act this way?"
"Why haven't you left yet?"
"Are you being a good, godly wife?"
"Have you tried harder to submit or forgive?"

These questions may sound spiritual. But in the context of coercive
control, they function as barriers to safety. They assume mutual
responsibility in situations where power is uneven. They misunderstand fear
as rebellion. They teach survivors that disclosure leads to scrutiny, not
protection. Abuse is not a marriage problem to solve; it is a safety issue to
address.

Why Reconciliation Cannot Come First

One of the most dangerous misconceptions inside faith communities is
the belief that reconciliation is always the highest goal. Reconciliation
without safety is not biblical—It is dangerous.

True reconciliation requires:
- Accountability.
- Sustained change.
- External oversight.
- Demonstrated repentance over time.

Anything less is pressure disguised as faith.

When churches rush reconciliation, they often place survivors back into
harm while calling it obedience. Jesus never prioritized unity over
protection.

What Churches Must Learn to Do Instead

Churches do not need to diagnose abuse. They do need to respond appropriately when it is disclosed.

That begins with four essential shifts:
1. Believe first; assess second.
    a. Listening without interrogation is not naïve. It is protective. Belief creates safety. Assessment can follow.
2. Watch patterns, not personalities.
    a. Charm, service, and consistency do not negate harm. Patterns over time matter more than presentation.
3. Prioritize safety over optics.
    a. Protecting reputation at the expense of life is not neutrality. It is harm.
4. Build referral pathways before disclosure happens.
    a. Churches should already know:
        i. Local domestic violence resources
        ii. Trauma-informed counselors
        iii. Emergency safety planning options

Waiting until a woman discloses to figure this out is too late.

Training Strengthens Faith — It Does Not Undermine It

Some churches resist abuse training because they fear it will secularize ministry or weaken spiritual authority. The opposite is true. Training strengthens discernment. It protects leaders from causing harm unintentionally. It honors the biblical mandate to protect the vulnerable. No church would place volunteers in children's ministry without training. Marriage counseling and abuse response deserve the same seriousness.

What It Would Have Changed for Me

If even one leader had known how to respond early—three years into my marriage—my story would have unfolded differently. Not necessarily with a faster exit. But with less isolation. With clearer boundaries. With safer planning. With support instead of self-doubt.

Education does not remove free will; it removes unnecessary suffering.

FOR CHURCH LEADERS –

A Practical Call to Action

If you want your church to be safer for survivors:
- Establish clear disclosure protocols.
- Create partnerships with licensed professionals.
- Normalize conversations about coercive control.
- Teach that abuse is not limited to physical violence.

You do not need to have all the answers. You need to be prepared enough not to cause harm.

FOR SURVIVORS –

If You Were Asked the Wrong Questions

If you were blamed, questioned, minimized, or spiritually corrected when you reached out, that was not God's design.

- That was a system operating without training.
- Your safety matters more than appearances.
- Your fear deserves respect.
- Your timeline is valid.

You were not asking the church to choose sides.
You were asking it to protect life.

CHAPTER ELEVEN – IF YOU ARE STILL THERE

If you are reading this while still inside a marriage that feels confusing, heavy, or unsafe, I want to speak to you gently.

Not urgently.

Not loudly.

Not with demands or instructions.

Just honestly.

You are not imagining things. If your body tightens before conversations even begin, if your words feel rehearsed before they're spoken, if your peace depends on how well you anticipate someone else's mood—that is not spiritual sensitivity. That is survival. And survival does not mean you are failing.

Delayed Leaving Is Not Weakness

Many women believe they are doing something wrong because they haven't left yet.

They hear questions like:
- Why haven't you done anything?
- If it's really that bad, why are you still there?
- What's keeping you?

Those questions misunderstand how danger works. Leaving is not a single decision; it is a series of calculations.

- Safety.
- Children.
- Finances.
- Health.
- Support systems.
- Timing.

You may understand the truth long before you are able to act on it. That does not make you disobedient. It makes you wise. Clarity often arrives before capacity. And capacity takes time.

Physical Abuse Does Not Require a Fist

Many survivors minimize their experiences because they were taught a narrow definition of physical abuse.
If you have told yourself:

- "It wasn't physical abuse because he never closed his fist."
- "He never hit my face."
- "It wasn't like what other people go through."

I want to say this clearly:

- Physical abuse includes intimidation.
- Blocking exits.
- Grabbing arms.
- Standing over you.
- Cornering you.
- Using his body to make you feel trapped.
- Restraining. Shoving. Looming. Choking. Throwing.

Your nervous system does not need bruises to register danger. Fear is information. And your body has been telling the truth long before language arrived.

Faith Was Never Meant to Cost You Yourself

If scripture has been used to silence you instead of protect you, that is not biblical leadership. If submission has been framed as endurance of harm, that is not covenant. If patience has been demanded without accountability, that is not love. Jesus does not require you to disappear in order to be faithful.

You Are Not Responsible for Another Adult's Choices

One of the heaviest lies survivors carry is the belief that they could fix this if they just tried harder.

- If they were calmer.
- If they were more patient.
- If they prayed differently.
- If they submitted more completely.

But abuse is not a communication problem. It is a control problem.

- You did not cause it.
- You cannot cure it.
- And it's not yours to manage alone.

Love does not require self-betrayal.

Leaving is not the only courageous thing a woman does.

Awareness is courageous too: learning quietly, gathering information, creating internal boundaries, preparing without announcing. You are allowed to take steps that no one else can see yet. You are allowed to move at the speed of safety. And you are allowed to trust yourself even if others don't understand your timeline.

FOR CHURCH LEADERS –

If Survivors Read This and Feel Seen

If a woman recognizes herself in this chapter, it means she has likely been surviving silently for a long time. Your role is not to accelerate her decisions. It is to slow your assumptions.

Survivors need:

- Belief without interrogation.
- Safety without judgment.
- Space to plan without spiritual guilt.

Urgency for leadership can increase danger. Presence decreases it.

FOR SURVIVORS –

A Final Word Just for You

If you are still smiling in public while unraveling privately, you are not fake.

- You are adaptive.

If you still love God but feel confused about marriage, you are not faithless.

- You are discerning.

If you are not ready to leave yet, you are not failing.

- You are preparing.

And when the time comes—whether soon or much later—you will not walk alone. Even if it feels that way right now.

I know.

Because I was there too.

FINAL CHAPTER – I STILL BELIEVE

I didn't write this book because I stopped believing in the church. I wrote it because I still do. I believe in the power of community when it is trained to protect, not just comfort. I believe in faith that does more than soothe—it intervenes. I believe in a God who does not ask women to disappear in order to stay holy. And I believe the church can become safer than it has been. But belief alone is not enough.

What I Know Now That I Didn't Then

- I know now that abuse thrives where confusion is spiritualized.
- I know now that silence is often mistaken for strength.
- I know now that many churches did not fail me because they didn't care—they failed me because they didn't know what to do, and they were afraid to admit it.
- I know now that apology after the fact, while sincere, is not the same as preparation before harm.
- And I know now that systems do not change by accident.

They change because someone tells the truth and refuses to carry it quietly anymore.

I Didn't Lose My Faith. I Reclaimed It.

There was never a moment when God left me.
- Not when I was confused.
- Not when I stayed longer than people thought I should.
- Not when I carried illness, fear, and responsibility all at once.
- Not when I left quietly.
- Not when the backlash came.
- Not when I slept more than I lived for a while.

Jesus was present in every season—especially the ones where I felt unseen by people who should have known how to respond. My faith didn't break. It matured. It became less performative and more honest. Less about appearances and more about truth. Less about endurance and more about life.

I still love ministry. I still serve. I still smile. But now my smile comes from peace, not pressure.

What I Hope the Church Will Choose Next

I hope churches choose training over tradition when tradition fails to protect. I hope leaders choose humility over certainty when a woman's story doesn't resolve neatly. I hope prayer becomes a beginning, not a substitute for action. I hope pastors and leaders learn to sit with complexity without pushing women toward premature reconciliation or unsafe patience. I hope the church becomes a place where a woman can say, "Something isn't right," and hear, "We will help you figure out what safety looks like."

Not later.

Now.

What I Hope Survivors Will Hear Clearly

If you see yourself in these pages, please know this:
- You are not late.
- You are not weak.
- You are not disobedient.
- You are not imagining things.
- Your body has been telling the truth all along.
- Healing does not erase your story—it integrates it.
- Leaving does not negate the love you showed.
- Staying does not mean you agreed to harm.
- And faith does not require you to lose yourself.

Why I Still Smile

- I smile because my home is quiet now.
- I smile because my children breathe easier.
- I smile because my nervous system no longer lives on adrenaline.
- I smile because my faith survived honesty.
- I smile because truth doesn't end hope—it restores it.

And I smile because I believe the church can learn if it is willing.

An Invitation, Not an Accusation

This book is not an indictment; it is an invitation.

- To learn.
- To train.
- To listen better.
- To respond sooner.
- To protect more courageously.

Because the church does not need to be perfect. It needs to be prepared. And women should not have to bleed invisibly in order to be believed.

I still believe.

And that belief is why I told the truth.

— End —

DISCUSSION GUIDE FOR CHURCH LEADERS

For pastors, elders, ministry leaders, staff, and faith-based counselors.

This guide is intended to help church leaders reflect honestly, learn responsibly, and respond more effectively to domestic abuse disclosures within faith communities. It is not designed to assign blame, but to increase preparedness, clarity, and safety. Leaders are encouraged to engage these questions slowly, prayerfully, and without defensiveness.

Before You Begin:

This discussion may surface discomfort. Discomfort is not failure—it is often the beginning of learning.

Abuse is not a hypothetical issue; survivors may already be present in your congregation.

These questions are not meant to be answered quickly; sit with them.

Section 1: Understanding the Blind Spot

1. In what ways has your church been trained to respond well to visible crises (addiction, homelessness, grief)?

2. How has your church been trained—or not trained—to respond to invisible crises like coercive control or domestic abuse?

3. What assumptions do you realize you may have held about abuse inside Christian marriages?

4. How might those assumptions unintentionally protect systems rather than people?

Reflection:
What does it cost a survivor when leaders are compassionate but unprepared?

Section 2: Abuse vs. Conflict

1. How does your leadership currently distinguish between marital conflict and abuse?

2. What behaviors described in the book challenged your understanding of what qualifies as physical or psychological abuse?

3. Why is it dangerous to require "proof" or visible injury before taking concerns seriously?

4. How might spiritual language unintentionally minimize harm when power dynamics are misunderstood?

Reflection:
How can churches learn to prioritize patterns over personalities?

Section 3: The Church's Response to Disclosure

1. What are the first questions you typically ask when someone discloses harm in their marriage?

2. How might questions like "Why haven't you left?" or "What are you doing to provoke this?" increase danger?

3. How can leaders respond with belief and safety without acting as investigators or judges?

4. What role should prayer play—and what role should it not replace?

Reflection:
What would a trauma-informed first response look like in your church?

Section 4: Training, Protocols, and Accountability

1. Does your church currently have:

   - Domestic abuse training for leaders?

   - Referral relationships with licensed professionals?

   - Clear safety protocols for disclosure?

2. If not, what has prevented this?

3. How might training strengthen—not undermine—biblical leadership?

4. What responsibility does the church have to children who are silently witnessing abuse?

Reflection:
What would it mean for your church to be prepared, not just well-intentioned?

Closing Reflection for Leaders

1. Where do you feel called to learn more?

2. Where might humility be required before confidence?

3. What is one concrete step your leadership can take within the next six months?

Reminder:
You do not need to have all the answers; you do need to be safe enough not to cause harm.

DISCUSSION GUIDE FOR SURVIVORS/SMALL GROUPS

For survivors, trusted support groups, and trauma-informed facilitators.

This guide is meant to be used gently; participants should never feel pressured to share personal details.

Listening is participation.
You may choose to journal privately instead of answering aloud.

Before You Begin:

You are allowed to engage this book at your own pace.
You are allowed to pause, skip sections, or step away.
Nothing needs to be decided as a result of this discussion.

Safety always comes first.

Section 1: Recognizing Yourself Without Shame

1. Which moments or patterns in the book felt familiar to you?

2. Were there places where you felt seen without feeling exposed?

3. In what ways have you adapted in order to survive?

Reflection:
What has your body learned that your mind may still be catching up to?

Section 2: Faith, Fear, and Confusion

1. Has faith ever felt heavy instead of healing in your relationship?

2. How has scripture been used—helpfully or harmfully—in your experience?

3. What messages about endurance or submission have caused confusion for you?

4. What does it feel like to hear that God does not require your erasure?

Reflection:
How might faith support safety instead of silence?

Section 3: Leaving, Staying, and Timing

1. What pressures have you felt around leaving—or not leaving?

2. How does the book describe delayed leaving differently than failure?

3. What factors would need to change for safety to increase in your life?

4. What does preparation look like for you right now?

Reflection:
What would it mean to honor your timeline without shame?

Section 4: Healing and Rebuilding

1. How does the book describe healing beyond emotions—especially in the body?

2. What reactions surprised you about trauma and recovery?

3. Where do you feel exhaustion that hasn't yet had permission to rest?

4. What supports feel safe—or could become safe—with time?

Reflection:
What does peace feel like in your body, even in small moments?

Section 5: Moving Forward Gently

1. What truths do you want to hold onto after reading this book?

2. What lies about yourself are you ready to release?

3. How can you practice self-compassion in this season?

4. What would it mean to trust your instincts again?

Reflection:
What does courage look like for you right now—not someday?

Closing Words for Survivors

You do not owe anyone a decision.

You do not need to prove harm.

You do not have to choose clarity and action at the same time.

Awareness is brave.
Rest is brave.
Truth is brave.

And you are allowed to take this journey one honest step at a time.

SPEAKING & EVENTS

Ginny Rucker speaks to churches, women's gatherings, and leadership teams on faith, clarity, and courageous truth.

For booking inquiries:
Speaking@ginnyrucker.com
www.ginnyrucker.com